7 Kinds Of Faith

Learning to Live by Faith

ABRAHAM JOHN

7 KINDS OF FAITH
Learning to Live by Faith

Copyright © 2016 by Abraham John

www.TheKingdomNetwork.org
email: info@thekingdomnetwork.org
1-800-558-5020

ISBN: 978-1-948330-30-5

All rights reserved. No part of this book may be reproduced or transmitted in any form or by any means, electronic or mechanical—including photocopying, recording, or by any information storage and retrieval system without permission in writing from the author. Please direct inquiries to mim@maximpact.org.

Unless otherwise noted, all Scripture were taken from the New King James Version®. Copyright © 1982 by Thomas Nelson. Used by permission. All rights reserved. Scriptures marked YLT are taken from the Young's Literal Translation. Public Domain.

TABLE OF CONTENTS

Chapter 1: Why Faith?	5
Chapter 2: The 7 Different Kinds of Faith	17
Chapter 3: Steps to Living by Faith	37
Chapter 4: Why Our Faith Doesn't Seem to Work	45
Chapter 5: Putting Your Faith to Work	55
Chapter 6: It is All by Faith	77
Questions	99
More Books & Resources	103

CHAPTER 1

Why Faith?

"For whatever is not from faith is sin."
Romans 14:23b

Do you know that whatever does not come from faith is sin? If we are not living by faith, we are in sin. There is only one way to live our Christian life, and that is to live by faith.

Living by faith is not just for those who are in ministry, but for every believer in Christ. The Bible says the "just" shall live by faith. If you are a just person (justified by faith in Christ) you are supposed to be living by faith.

> Hebrews 10:38, "**Now** the **just shall live by faith**; but if *anyone* draws back, My soul

has no pleasure in him." (Habakkuk 2:4; Romans 1:17; Galatians 3:11)

The Bible calls the faith we received from God, "most holy faith."

> But you, beloved, building yourselves up on your **most holy faith**, praying in the Holy Spirit. Jude 1:20

God has entrusted you and me with something so precious: the most holy faith. It is very important to note that when the Bible talks about the faith that is given to us, it uses the term *most holy faith*. There are other holy things and truths that God has given us, but there is only one described as *most* holy, and that is our faith.

I believe the reason that phrase is used to describe our faith is because there is a possibility that our faith can get corrupted or defiled. When there is something most holy and precious we will take care and protect it better.

It is most holy because it is the very substance that God used to create the universe. You and I carry the same substance in our spirit. So imagine the value and the power we carry within ourselves.

Since we entered this new season—the year of God's glory for the body of Christ—He has prompted me to teach about faith. In order to live in God's glory we need to learn to live and operate in faith.

WHY FAITH?

Many believers think they live by faith, but in reality, they are living by what they see with their natural eyes, based on their emotions and immediate circumstances, depending only on what their own abilities can produce. If Christians live based on what their own abilities can produce, then they are no better off than an unbeliever!

Faith is not something that you *feel,* nor is it an *emotion.* This is very important to understand. Many people confuse faith with their emotions, and do not walk by faith during the times when they feel as though they never had any faith.

Faith is a substance; it is an invisible substance—it is a God—kind of substance (Hebrews 11:1). It is the very substance He used to create the universe.

Amazingly, faith is a quality of your spirit which He deposited into your inner being. *You can use this substance any time you choose, regardless of how you feel at any given moment.*

To live by faith means your emotions or circumstances do not dictate how you live. You live with a heavenly perspective and with a heavenly vision.

Faith is the link between the natural and the supernatural, the visible and the invisible.

God never intended for you to live based on what you can do in your own ability, but based on His ability—His unlimited resources, wisdom, and grace.

There is only one way to please God and to fulfill your purpose, and that is to walk and live by faith (Hebrews 11:6).

If you are living by your emotions and based on your circumstances; then you are either living in your flesh, or you have gone through a tremendous attack from the enemy in your faith, and you have strayed away from the faith-track.

God wants to restore your faith so that He can pour into your life everything He has in store for you.

This book is intended to help you to restore your life of faith, by enabling you to take baby steps until you are fully restored and become a giant in faith toward God.

The Devil does not want you to live by faith. He hates faith because it is one of the qualities he cannot operate in.

This is not a study about little faith, great faith, or mustard seed faith. You have already heard of those many times. This is an in-depth study of God's Word about the different *kinds* of faith He has given to us so we can be thoroughly equipped to do every good work He has created us to do.

Everything in this universe and in our life operates based on a law that was established by God. The Bible calls faith a law. Faith is a spiritual law, just like work is.

We are not supposed to be operating by the law of work alone, but by works that the law of faith produces. Faith won't function without works. Our works need to be birthed from the faith we have. Every time we depend on our work alone to earn anything from God we bring ourselves under a curse.

Everything we do in the New Testament is supposed to be appropriated and activated by the law of faith. It must begin by faith, and then works; and not vice versa.

> "Where *is* boasting then? It is excluded. By what law? Of works? No, but by the law of faith. Therefore we conclude that a man is justified by faith apart from the deeds of the law." (Romans 3:27-28)

We need to change some of our ways of thinking and the methods we were operating in last year, in order to live out this new season God has for us. If we continue to operate the same way we did in the past year, we will miss the blessings and favor that He has for us in this new season. We will just continue in the same problems and challenges of last year, bringing these into this New Year. This is not God's plan for us!

We are now in an accelerated season of God's purpose and timing for our lives.

Many believers have no understanding about this most holy faith. I did not always know that there were seven different kinds of faith. I only knew about one kind of faith, the faith that comes by hearing the Word of God. I taught and even wrote about it; but when God opened my understanding about the different kinds of faith, it totally changed my perception about the topic.

The devil is not after your health, wealth, or any other possession you have; he is after your faith. He is after your mind and your words. He attacks your faith in God's Word and His character. He influences you to think like the people in the world, and to speak words contrary to God's word, and to take things into your own hands, trusting in yourself instead of trusting God.

The Pitfall of the Faith Movement

In one of my family's Bible and prayer times, we were reading Hebrews chapter 11, better known as the hall of fame of the people of faith. Hebrews chapter 11 is an overview of the Old Testament, and talks about what people did through their faith in God.

What surprised me is that I could not find a single verse about a person who used their faith to obtain material benefits. They all did great exploits by faith.

I was grieved in my spirit to see that many people who follow today's faith teachings, use their faith to obtain a better life—or luxury life.

In the Bible, people rejected a better life here on earth, believing and looking forward to something better in the life to come. They looked for a better city or a country whose founder and maker was God (Hebrews 11:10, 16; 13:14). They denied the fleeting glory of material possessions of this earth in comparison to the eternal reward they were looking forward to obtaining in the life to come.

The Bible talks about two kinds of faith people. There are different kinds of lifestyles that God calls people to live. Whichever category we belong in, we should be happy and satisfied with. That is why Paul says that each one should remain in the state that they were called (1 Corinthians 7:20, 24).

The same God and Holy Spirit who was upon David was also upon Elijah and Elisha. But David lived in a palace, wearing fine linen, and eating the best food, with all the luxury that was available; while Elijah on the other hand, wore animal's skin, lived in caves or dens, and ate miracle food provided by God each day.

> Hebrews 11:33-39, Who through faith subdued kingdoms, worked righteousness, obtained promises, stopped the mouths of lions, quenched the violence of fire, escaped the edge of the sword, out of weakness were made strong, became valiant in battle, turned to flight the armies of the aliens. Women received their dead raised to life again. Others were tortured, not accepting

deliverance, that they might obtain a better resurrection. Still others had trial of mockings and scourgings, yes, and of chains and imprisonment. They were stoned, they were sawn in two, were tempted, were slain with the sword. They wandered about in sheepskins and goatskins, being destitute, afflicted, tormented—of whom the world was not worthy. They wandered in deserts and mountains, *in* dens and caves of the earth. And all these, having obtained a good testimony through faith, did not receive the promise.

When I read the above verses they really touched my spirit. We do not usually hear those preached these days. We mostly hear messages about Abraham, Joseph, and David. But those people who were destitute, afflicted, tormented, and the like, *were people of faith.*

Imagine someone standing up in your church today, giving a testimony that they have faith, but live in a cave in Cambodia for the sake of the gospel; or they just bought a goatskin to wear, and they are destitute. Our minds would have a hard time comprehending or accepting such a testimony. We may immediately pass judgment; inwardly thinking those people must have gone wrong somewhere concerning their "faith" in God and His Word.

But this is truth, and is truly biblical. We need David as well as Elijah and Elisha in the kingdom! We need

John the Baptist, who wore camel's hair for clothing (Matthew 3:4); and we also need Joseph of Arimathea, a rich and prominent council member, who waited for the kingdom of God (Mark 15:43).

When the body of Christ embraces these two different streams of faith and anointing, and learns to balance these, we will see a tremendous demonstration of God's power and glory.

I am in no way justifying poverty. Poverty is demonic. Elijah and Elisha were not poor. They deliberately denied the passions and possessions of this world in order to focus more on their calling and relationship with God—that was their priority. Because of their level of faith and relationship with God, they could speak something and watch it come to pass exactly as they said it would.

People who use their faith only to obtain material things have corrupted their most holy faith and shipwrecked their life. Many in the word of faith movement have misinformed us that if we are not living a certain kind of lifestyle in relation to material wealth, then we are not spiritual enough or do not have enough faith. That is not true according to the Bible.

> James 2:5, "Listen, my beloved brethren: Has God not chosen the poor of this world *to be* rich in faith and heirs of the kingdom which He promised to those who love Him?"

James did not say concerning the poor that there is something wrong with their faith.

> 1 Timothy 1:18-20, "This charge I commit to you, son Timothy, according to the prophecies previously made concerning you, that by them you may wage the good warfare, having faith and a good conscience, which some having rejected, concerning the faith have suffered shipwreck, of whom are Hymenaeus and Alexander, whom I delivered to Satan that they may learn not to blaspheme."

The verse above says some people have shipwrecked their lives concerning their faith. This happens when someone loses their focus and begins to use faith for only obtaining a better life here and now.

I have discovered that wherever there is a religious spirit, it justifies poverty as a spiritual attainment. This is not biblical. However choosing to remain poor by denying the riches of this world even though you could have had them, is a whole different thing. The apostle Paul is an example of this. He could have had anything he wanted, yet he abstained from overindulging anything of the world in order to be an example for other ministers.

> 1 Corinthians 4:11, To the present hour we both hunger and thirst, and we are poorly clothed, and beaten, and homeless.

Can you believe the above verse is the personal testimony of the most influential apostle who ever lived? Though he died almost 2,000 years ago, he is still changing lives and impacting nations. It was not the style of clothing or the abundance of goods he possessed, but the life he lived in the spirit that made the difference.

As I said, until recently, I thought there was only one kind of faith—the faith that comes by hearing. I believed that until we hear from God there is no faith, and if someone stepped out in faith without hearing God they were destined to fail. But God opened my understanding to see that there are other kinds of faith; where people stepped out in faith based on the knowledge they had of God, and saw miraculous things happen. I will explain all of these types of faith in detail in this book.

Studying about faith is very important, because without faith it is impossible to please God, and because we can wreck our faith if we are not careful.

CHAPTER 2

The 7 Different Kinds of Faith

1. Faith That Comes by Hearing

> Romans 10:17, "So then faith *comes* by hearing, and hearing by the word of God."

The first kind of faith is that which comes when we hear the Word of God being preached or read. We read in the letter to the Romans about faith in relation to receiving salvation.

When people hear the gospel preached, faith is birthed in their spirit, and they are open to acknowledge their need of a Savior. The result of this faith is to receive Jesus into their lives as their Savior and Lord. The end of that faith is eternal salvation (1 Peter 1:9).

Do you remember the day and moment you were saved?

It was the most exciting moment and day of our lives! I can still remember the encounter I had with God. It was nothing dramatic, but it was a key moment in my walk with the Lord. I did not have a dramatic experience when I was saved.

I did not have any miraculous deliverance or see lightning from heaven. I was maybe twelve or thirteen years old and attended a convention our church did yearly in my hometown in India. I had gone to hear a guest speaker who came to speak at the convention that year.

When the guest speaker gave an altar call, something prompted me to go forward and receive prayer. His preaching produced faith in my heart.

I was drawn by the anointing on that man, though I did not realize what faith or anointing was at that time. That was the first experience I can remember that I had with God.

Then when I was sixteen years old, I gave my life to Jesus, and was water baptized. That same year, I was also baptized in the Holy Spirit. When I was eighteen years old, I left my home to obey the call of God on my life.

There will come a time in each one of our lives where we have the option to choose to live by faith or to live by trusting in our own reasoning.

Some choose to live by faith and trust God, and others choose to live by their circumstances and reasoning. Faith is living by what you see in your spirit, while living by reasoning is choosing to live by what you see with your natural eyes.

My dream was to be an electronic engineer, but around seventeen or eighteen years old I felt in my heart that I needed to go to a Bible school; which was a three-day journey by train from my hometown. I am so happy that I obeyed God rather than my reasoning and the opinions of other people who were close to me—some of them being my own family members. Living by faith is more exciting and adventurous than any other adventure you could experience.

By faith you tap into the unlimited resources of God. When you live by your reasoning—you depend on natural resources, things that you can produce on your own—these are always limited.

It has been twenty-five years since I left my home, and God has never let me down even once. Though the enemy attacked me on every side and I have been through hell a few times, He has proven Himself faithful again and again.

Faith that comes by hearing God's Word works not only for salvation, but even after you are saved. When you hear the revelatory Word being preached, faith will surface in your heart to take appropriate action.

> Ephesians 2:8-9, "For by grace you have been saved through faith, and that not of yourselves; *it is* the gift of God, not of works, lest anyone should boast."

God, who is rich in mercy, wanted to show forth the abundance of His grace toward us, which is why the Bible says, "The law was given by Moses, but grace and truth came through Jesus Christ" (John 1:17). God gives grace, and when the gospel of grace is being preached, faith gets birthed in our spirit. When grace and faith combine together in the heart of a person, these produce salvation.

> The grace that brings salvation has appeared to all men (Titus 2:11).

Once you are saved, never depend on the works of the law. If you do, you will bring yourselves under a curse. Unfortunately, many honest believers are operating under a curse in different areas of their lives without knowing the root of it. Many are confused between the Old and New Testaments, and they take one verse from the Old Testament and another from the New Testament and then try to obey them all.

> Galatians 3:10, For as many as are of the works of the law are under the curse; for it

is written, 'Cursed *is* everyone who does not continue in all things which are written in the book of the law, to do them.'

One of the main reasons why believers come under curses is because they try to obey the Old Testament law that God does no longer require. Either you obey them all or leave them alone. If you obey most and break one, you bring yourselves under the curse (James 2:10). The truth is, no one could keep all the laws of the Old Testament because of their sinful nature. This is why God had to send Jesus to fulfill the law for us, so that the blessing of those who obey the law might come upon us (Romans 8:3-4).

2. The Measure of Faith

God has given the measure of faith to everyone of us. Paul the Apostle wrote:

> Romans 12:3-8, "For I say, through the grace given to me, to everyone who is among you, not to think *of himself* more highly than he ought to think, but to think soberly, as **God has dealt to each one a measure of faith.**
>
> For as we have many members in one body, but all the members do not have the same function, so we, *being* many, are one body in Christ, and individually members of one another.

> Having then gifts differing according to the grace that is given to us, *let us use them:* if prophecy, *let us prophesy* in proportion to our faith; or ministry, *let us use it* in *our* ministering; he who teaches, in teaching; he who exhorts, in exhortation; he who gives, with liberality; he who leads, with diligence; he who shows mercy, with cheerfulness."

When you are born again you become a member of the Body of Christ. Each member has a unique gift and function, just like each member of our physical body has a unique function and position.

In order for us to fulfill our responsibility as a member of the Body of Christ, God takes us to another level by depositing some special gifts into us. He also deposits a measure of faith into our spirit to operate that gift.

That measure of faith is the empowerment to operate the gifts. This faith does not come by hearing. It comes as a deposit into your spirit. The more you exercise the gifts, the stronger this faith becomes. Every believer has received this faith.

It is also important to understand that we believe in a triune God: Father, Son, and Holy Spirit. Though our God is one God, He manifests Himself in three different persons. Each gives different gifts to people:

> 1 Corinthians 12:4-6, There are diversities of gifts, but the **same Spirit.** There

are differences of ministries, but the **same Lord**. And there are diversities of activities, but it is the **same God** who works all in all.

The above verses always leave a strong impression in my heart. The Bible says there are diversities of gifts, but the same Spirit.

The Holy Spirit gives gifts. Some of His gifts are mentioned in 1 Corinthians 12:7-11, "But the manifestation of the Spirit is given to each one for the profit *of all:* for to one is given the word of wisdom through the Spirit, to another the word of knowledge through the same Spirit, to another faith by the same Spirit, to another gifts of healings by the same Spirit, to another the working of miracles, to another prophecy, to another discerning of spirits, to another *different* kinds of tongues, to another the interpretation of tongues. But one and the same Spirit works all these things, distributing to each one individually as He wills."

There are different kinds of ministries, but the same Lord. There is only one Lord, and that is our Lord and Savior Jesus Christ who gives ministries to people.

> Ephesians 4:7-8, 11, But to each one of us grace was given according to the measure of Christ's gift. Therefore He says: 'When He ascended on high, He led captivity captive, and gave gifts to men'...And He Himself gave some *to be* apostles, some prophets, some evangelists, and some pastors and teachers.

It is Christ Who gives these ministry gifts to His church.

There are diversities of activities, but the same God. What are the activities God gave to people?

Every human being is born with a natural ability or gift. Because God is love He has blessed them regardless of what they believe. Some have an ability to sing, draw, and do other creative things.

They do not have to be Christians to operate those gifts. In order to operate the gift that is in them, people need to exercise faith. For example, if a singer needs to get up on the stage to perform, he or she needs to operate by faith, believing that it's going to go well.

Then, when a person is Born Again, God gives them more gifts. When a person is baptized in the Holy Spirit they receive more gifts again. Imagine how many gifts we each possess!

Sadly, most believers do not discover and develop their gifts. Despite being advantaged as we are when compared to the people of this world, many times we are not as productive as the people in the world. Instead of discovering and developing our gifts, we wait around for God to do everything for us—when He has already done more than we even realize.

In Romans chapter 12, Paul lists the different kinds of activities or gifts God gave to us; and said we need to function according to the measure of faith God gave to us:

> Romans 12:6-8, Having then gifts differing according to the grace that is given to us, *let us use them:* if prophecy, *let us prophesy* in proportion to our faith; or ministry, *let us use it* in *our* ministering; he who teaches, in teaching; he who exhorts, in exhortation; he who gives, with liberality; he who leads, with diligence; he who shows mercy, with cheerfulness.

Whether you realize it or not, you have a measure of faith in you. There is not a single believer who has not received that measure of faith!

3. The Gift of Faith

> 1 Corinthians 12:9, To another faith by the same Spirit, to another gifts of healings by the same Spirit.

There is a different level of faith that the Holy Spirit gives as He chooses to certain people. It is called the gift of faith.

This faith does not come by hearing God's Word, nor does it come with our salvation as the measure of faith. This is a supernatural level of faith that causes a person to do extraordinary things that would not be possible naturally. Not everyone possesses this kind of faith, only a few.

The Bible also calls it the spirit of faith (2 Corinthians 4:13). When this faith moves in the heart of people, they feel they can do things supernaturally that they could never do on their own. People who have the gift of faith can do the impossible. They do not necessarily need to hear from God in order to operate this faith.

Elijah told King Ahab that there would not be any rain or dew from heaven until he spoke. We do not see God telling Elijah to go and say this to the king. He was operating under the gift of faith.

> 1 Kings 17:1, And Elijah the Tishbite, of the inhabitants of Gilead, said to Ahab, '*As* the Lord God of Israel lives, before whom I stand, there shall not be dew nor rain these years, except at my word.'

Wow! That is the gift of faith.

Another example we see is Joshua telling the sun to stand still. Whether the sun stopped moving or the earth stopped, there was no sunset for an extra day. There was an extra twenty-four hours of *daytime* for them to finish the battle. Here is how the power of the gift of faith manifested:

> Joshua 10:12-14, Then Joshua spoke to the Lord in the day when the Lord delivered

up the Amorites before the children of Israel, and he said in the sight of Israel:

'Sun, stand still over Gibeon;
And Moon, in the Valley of Aijalon.'
So the sun stood still,
And the moon stopped,
Till the people had revenge
Upon their enemies.

Is this not written in the Book of Jasher? So the sun stood still in the midst of heaven, and did not hasten to go *down* for about a whole day. And there has been no day like that, before it or after it, that the Lord heeded the voice of a man; for the Lord fought for Israel.

This is the faith that raises the dead. There is no other power that can withstand the power of the gift of faith!

4. The Faith of God

This is one of the most important faiths every believer should choose to operate in on a moment-by-moment basis.

God has revealed to us one of His secrets (Psalm 25:14). He used this faith when He created the universe. This is why faith is called a mystery in the Bible (1Timothy 3:9).

> Mark 11:22-23 (YLT), And Jesus answering saith to them, 'Have faith of God; for verily I say to you, that whoever may say to this mount, Be taken up, and be cast into the sea, and may not doubt in his heart, but may believe that the things that he saith do come to pass, it shall be to him whatever he may say.'

The above verse says have faith of God. What is the faith of God? It is the kind of faith you release by speaking. Words are one of the most creative forces in the universe.

In the above verse, Jesus is telling us to have the faith of God. When God needs something done, all that He needs to do is speak. He has given us the same capacity to operate at His level, by speaking words that are creative or destructive.

Many of the misfortunes we experience are the direct result of words that we have spoken. If we do not like the harvest we are receiving then we need to change the words we have been speaking.

The Faith (or Word of Faith) Movement was birthed out of the revelation of this faith from Mark 11:22-23. Out of it came the "name it and claim it" theology. People have taken this type of faith to an extreme, and they began to use it for personal material gain. Out of this came the term *prosperity gospel*. This is not a biblically sound doctrine of the New Testament church. As long as we use this faith for the right reason and stay balanced, we will reap its benefits.

After finishing Bible school in India I joined Youth With A Mission (YWAM) to go through their discipleship course. I went to Nepal with a team as part of our outreach. I was twenty-four years of age at that time, and I had never flown in an airplane before, because I did not have any money.

We were stationed in Kathmandu, Nepal, which is surrounded by mountains and we were close to the airport. From the facility we were staying at I could see the airplanes landing and taking off from the other side of the mountain.

One afternoon, as I was watching an airplane taking off I spoke to myself and said, "Next year by this time, I will fly in an airplane." That's all I said.

Naturally there was no possibility that I could fly in an airplane. But God honored my faith, and did a series of miracles; and the next year around the same time I flew to the United States of America to further my studies. I was not flying in a little airplane taking a short trip. I was flying across the ocean in one of the largest airplanes around.

How could something like that happen? That is the power of the faith of God.

You do not necessarily need to hear from God to operate in this faith. This faith can be based on the knowledge you already have of God.

David is another example of a person who operated in this kind of faith. When Goliath came against Israel and challenged them for forty days, the news about it reached David's ears.

Based on the knowledge and experience he had with God, he decided to face the giant on his own. When Saul questioned his ability to conquer the giant—who had been a man of war from his youth—David testified of the experiences he had in killing the lion and the bear. Then he said something powerful:

> 1 Samuel 17:37, Moreover David said, 'The Lord, who delivered me from the paw of the lion and from the paw of the bear, He will deliver me from the hand of this Philistine.' And Saul said to David, 'Go, and the Lord be with you!'

David exercised the faith of God and spoke of something happening before he could see it in the natural realm. His words ignited something in the spiritual realm and God gave him victory over the giant. We all know the rest of the story.

David made a covenant in his life that he would not speak a negative word when an adversary was in front of him.

> Psalm 39:1, "I said, 'I will guard my ways, Lest I sin with my tongue; I will restrain my mouth with a muzzle, While the wicked are before me.'"

What if each of us made a covenant with our mouth to not speak anything negative about ourselves or others? I believe we would see tremendous breakthroughs that we have been waiting to see.

Jesus said in Mark 11: 24 that we shall have whatever we say. So, if we are to operate by the faith of God, then we really need to make a commitment not to speak negative confessions.

Jesus calls this *great faith*. For example, when a centurion came to Him for the healing of his servant, Jesus marveled at the faith of this man—who was not even a disciple or Jewish—who believed in the power of spoken words that release faith and authority (Matthew 8:5-10).

5. Justified by Faith

> Romans 5:1, Therefore, having been **justified by faith**, we have peace with God through our Lord Jesus Christ.

When a person puts their faith in Jesus Christ and His work on the cross, he or she immediately activates another kind of faith: the faith of our father Abraham.

It is a generational faith we inherit because of the faith and obedience of Abraham (Galatians 3:6-9).

God declares that person *just* or *righteous* regardless of what they did or did not do.

This faith is different from the measure of faith, gift of faith, or any other kind of faith we receive. This is the faith of our father, Abraham, which is imputed to us through Jesus Christ.

> Romans 4:11-12, And he received the sign of circumcision, a seal of the righteousness of the faith which *he had while still* uncircumcised, that he might be the father of all those who believe, though they are uncircumcised, that righteousness might be imputed to them also, and the father of circumcision to those who not only *are* of the circumcision, **but who also walk in the steps of the faith which our father Abraham *had while still* uncircumcised**.

> Romans 4:16, Therefore *it is* of faith that *it might be* according to grace, so that the promise might be sure to all the seed, not only to those who are of the law, but also to those who are of the **faith of Abraham**, who is the father of us all.

We need to live by this faith every day for the rest of our lives. The moment we tend to depend on anything else we do to be accepted by or to please God, we fall from grace and slip back into the law (Galatians 5:4). And when we are under the law, we are under a curse (Galatians 3:10).

This is why the Bible says in four different places, "The just shall live by faith." There is only one way to live the Christian life, and that is to live by faith.

When we are not living by faith, it is not pleasing to the Lord (Hebrews 11:6). The Bible says whatever is not of faith is sin (Romans 14:23b).

Paul explains in Galatians 2:20 how he lived. "I have been crucified with Christ; it is no longer I who live, but Christ lives in me; **and the *life* which I now live in the flesh I live by faith in the Son of God, who loved me and gave Himself for me**."

6. Faith for Charitable Works

> James 2:14-17, "What *does it* profit, my brethren, if someone says he has faith but does not have works? Can faith save him? If a brother or sister is naked and destitute of daily food, and one of you says to them, 'Depart in peace, be warmed and filled,' but you do not give them the things which are needed for the body, what *does it* profit? Thus also faith by itself, if it does not have works, is dead."

If you really are to love or help someone, you need to operate in faith. What good is having faith if you don't do anything with it? James spoke to believers who claimed to be people of faith and had nothing to show as the result of their faith. He admonished them to show their faith with appropriate works. God gives you faith to help someone and to be a blessing to others.

I remember the day when I felt that God was asking me to help the orphans and destitute children in India. I was traveling in a three-wheel taxi and I saw a little girl, maybe three years old, wearing torn underwear and playing in the mud on the side of the road. I had seen such children many times before. But this time what I saw really touched my heart, and I began to cry. When I looked over at my friend who was traveling with me, he was also crying. I heard the voice of God saying, "You need to do something about this."

The only way I knew to help them was to start an orphanage. At that time, our ministry did not have much money, but by faith we looked around and found an old house to rent. My friend and I had to chase monkeys and bats out of the building to clean it, and it took us a week to clean. I was staying in a hotel and I did not have money to check out unless God did a miracle. He did many miracles, and we opened our orphanage with seven destitute children.

It's been fourteen years now, and those children and many others have been raised in our children's home.

Some of them are married now, others are in ministry and working, while some are still in school.

Anything you do for God has to originate in faith. If you can do it by yourself with what you have then you do not need God.

7. Faith That Overcomes the World

> 1 John 5:4, For whatever is born of God overcomes the world. And this is the victory that has overcome the world—our faith.

Even if we have faith to move mountains and heal every sickness, we will jeopardize our life if we do not overcome this world.

There are so many examples around us and in the Bible of people who began their walk with God, and did not finish it. The passion and the lust of this world influenced them, and they fell prey to its temptations.

Samson is the best example from the Bible. There were very few people in the Bible who had the level of anointing which he did. Samson could do mighty deeds that nobody else ever did, but he could not overcome his own lust and passions, and it led to a tragic end for him.

Each believer is commanded to overcome the world. We need to be crucified to this world and its systems.

Unfortunately, in today's Christian world, the more you have of this world the more you are considered *blessed*. This is not necessarily true all of the time.

Paul says that one of his companions left the ministry because he saw something more attractive to do than following God. 2 Timothy 4:10a, "For Demas has forsaken me, having loved this present world, and has departed for Thessalonica." Maybe he had seen a business opportunity in Thessalonica.

Now that we have studied about faith, how do we live by faith? God has shown me seven practical steps that will help you to learn to live by faith.

CHAPTER 3

Steps to Living by Faith

In Hebrews chapter 11, we see a list of people who lived by faith. They obtained a great testimony about their faith from God. If you study the lives of those people listed in Hebrews 11, you will notice that they did not live their lives based on natural circumstances. They lived based on what they saw in their spirit.

For example, Moses rejected being called the son of Pharaoh's daughter, and left the luxury and influence he could have had in Egypt. He ran from Egypt because he saw the One Who is invisible. He had a vision about Christ and eternity. When compared to that, the fleeting momentary pleasures he could have had in Egypt were nothing. So he ran away and chose to suffer with God's people (Hebrews 11:24-27).

It is through faith and patience that we inherit God's promises (Hebrews 6:12). When we become God's children He gives us His promises as our inheritance. Those promises are like checks we receive from God. I wish it were easy to cash them like normal checks!

Just like He gave the promise to the children of Israel when they came out of Egypt, He gave promises to us.

He promised them a land that flows with milk and honey, but not everyone who heard the promise entered the Promised Land.

Only those who endured the tests and trials of the wilderness through faith and patience inherited the promise. I will explain in a nutshell the steps you can take to live by faith.

1. Discover the Will of God for Your Life

The first thing a new believer in Christ should be taught is to seek the kingdom of God and learn how His kingdom operates (Matthew 6:33). Please make sure you read the kingdom book series.

The second thing a believer in Christ should be taught is to how to discover their purpose. God gave us the faith to fulfill His purpose for our lives. But if we do not know our purpose, then we cannot use our faith effectively.

The following are the ways that you discover your purpose:

a. Prayer

God has not changed His way of communicating His will to us, which is through prayer.

I remember days and nights I used to spend in prayer, and gradually God began to impart His desires into my spirit. Before this, my desire was to become an electronic engineer.

b. The Holy Spirit

There is only one person in this whole universe who knows the will of God for your life, and that is the Holy Spirit.

1 Corinthians 2:9-12 states, " 'Eye has not seen, nor ear heard, nor have entered into the heart of man the things which God has prepared for those who love Him.'

But God has revealed *them* to us through His Spirit. For the Spirit searches all things, yes, the deep things of God.

For what man knows the things of a man except the spirit of the man which is in him? Even so no one knows the things of God except the Spirit of God.

Now we have received, not the spirit of the world, but the Spirit who is from God, that we might know the things that have been freely given to us by God."

One of the main reasons why God gave us the Holy Spirit is to show us the things He has given us.

Many limit the Holy Spirit to an emotional experience or for His gifts, but never go deeper to know the things freely given to them by God.

"He who did not spare His own Son, but delivered Him up for us all, how shall He not with Him also freely give us all things?" (Romans 8:32)

God has an answer for every need we will ever have. Everything you need to fulfill God's purpose for your life, He has already prepared.

In order for us to receive what He has prepared for us, He gave us faith.

Have you ever asked the Holy Spirit to show you what God has in store for you? He knows the mind of God concerning our lives.

Make friends with the Holy Spirit. The reason most people do not receive any help from the Holy Spirit is because they do not ask Him.

Imagine, God sent a person to be with you and in you and to guide you, and you never talk to Him. How would you feel if someone you love was with you but never talked to you? That is the way the Holy Spirit feels with many of us. We never even acknowledge that He is with us.

c. The Word of God

The more you read and meditate on God's Word, the better you will hear the voice of God; because when God speaks, He sounds like His Word.

The Word is the revealed will of God. If we have no regard for what is already revealed, then He will not reveal what is hidden.

Once you discover the will of God, then whatever you ask Him according to His will (for your life), He will grant you to your heart's desire.

The reason many of our prayers are not answered is because we ask amiss, because we are not asking according to His will concerning our lives (1 John 5:14).

2. Keep a Prayer Journal

The second thing you need to have is a prayer journal. In your prayer journal, write a list of things that you are believing God for this year.

The length of the list is not a problem for God. These should be practical and specific.

Please don't write things like, "I want to grow spiritually" or, "I would like to have more money," or "Peace," or, "Salvation of my loved ones." Those are not specific.

Instead write things like, "I want to pray fifteen minutes every day," or, "I would like to have a specific amount of income every month, or "Salvation of _____," and name someone specific. I have thirty-two items on my list for this year.

3. Lay hands on the list and pray over each item every day

Keep your prayer journal with you when you pray so that you can lay hands on it. As the Bible says in Matthew 18:19, (KJV), **"**Again I say unto you, That if two of you shall agree on earth as **touching** any thing that they shall ask, it shall be done for them of my Father which is in heaven."

4. Thank God for meeting/answering those needs

Thanking God as often as you can in advance as if He already answered the prayer, shows faith in our part.

5. Confess Pertinent Scriptures

Find Scriptures from the Bible that back up your requests, and pray those with your requests, and confess them so that you can hear it.

Confessing scriptures is one of the most powerful weapons against the enemy, and a tool to build our faith.

Whenever you find a verse that is connected to your need, write it down in your prayer journal and confess it daily.

6. Obey giving-prompts immediately

When you feel God telling you to do something, especially in the area of giving, please obey immediately.

Obedience is better than sacrifice. I have had several experiences in my life where everything turned around for the better when I obeyed God in the area of giving. There was one particular incident when I obeyed God in faith, which broke the spirit of poverty off my life. Everything we do today in this ministry goes back to that one seed I sowed in faith.

7. Pray for others and their needs as you would pray for yours

The golden rule says, "Therefore, whatever you want men to do to you, do also to them, for this is the Law and the Prophets" (Matthew 7:12).

I would say whatever you want God to do for you, help someone in the same area with what you have. You will see God do amazing things for you.

Many times breakthrough came to my life because I was willing to pray for someone when I was going through a difficult time.

When you are going through challenges is the least interesting time to minister to someone else. But, in the spirit, that is the best time to do so.

I have also experienced in ministry that whenever I did not feel like ministering or preaching, but did so out of obedience, God showed up, because it was birthed out of faith.

8. Live in obedience to His Word

Many are looking to receive extra-Biblical revelations—meaning they want God to speak to them, but they have no time to read their Bible.

> He told Joshua, "This Book of the Law shall not depart from your mouth, but you shall meditate in it day and night, that you may observe to do according to all that is written in it. For then you will make your way prosperous, and then you will have good success" (Joshua 1:8).

CHAPTER 4

Why Our Faith Doesn't Seem to Work

We have learned that we all receive faith when we are Born Again. However many are not benefitting from this, because they do not know how to operate in it.

In the following pages, we will learn how to put our faith to work, so we can receive everything God has for us, and be a blessing to others. Following are the reasons why our faith does not work.

1. Faith Without Works is Dead

Just like a coin has two sides, faith has two sides. One is natural and one is spiritual. We need to balance our focus on both sides in order to benefit from the faith God has given us.

When we study the miracles in the Bible, each one has a natural aspect and a spiritual aspect.

Some people only give importance to the spiritual and neglect the natural, so they do not receive much benefit from the faith God has given them. Others focus on the natural and not the spiritual, and they too miss out on what God has for them.

We all want to see more miracles in our lives and through our lives. God wants that for us also, but He is unable to manifest more miracles unless we cooperate with Him. Every miracle requires an action in the natural guided by the Holy Spirit.

> James 2:14, What *does it* profit, my brethren, if someone says he has faith but does not have works? Can faith save him?

This Scripture clearly tells us that faith, which is spiritual, that does not produce a corresponding action, which is natural, cannot save or help a person.

The greatest miracle we have received by faith is the salvation of our souls.

Even our salvation has a spiritual and natural aspect. Believing the gospel is the spiritual, and confessing it with our mouth is the natural. If a person only believes and never confesses, that person will not be saved (Romans 10:9).

If the people at the wedding of Cana never filled the jars with water, they would not have seen any miracles.

The people who were at the pool Bethesda had to jump into the water when the angel came and stirred the pool at certain times.

Naaman had to dip himself seven times in the Jordan River. If he had not done so, there would have been no cure for his leprosy.

Every time you ask God for a miracle, He will give you an instruction to do something in the natural. If you obey Him, you will see the miracle.

If not, you can pray all you want, shout all you want, or even fast, but you will not see the breakthrough any time soon.

Remember the story of Jericho? God commanded Joshua and the people to walk around the city once a day for six days, and on the seventh day to walk around it seven times and shout; then the wall fell.

If our faith does not have corresponding action then that faith is dead. Dead faith is a faith that is lacking action to prove it.

Your faith will be resurrected the moment you take the action which the Holy Spirit is telling you to do.

> James 2:26, For as the body without the spirit is dead, so faith without works is dead also.

2. Faith that Works by Love

If our faith is to work, then it has be mixed with love. Many times the reason our faith does not produce the result we are hoping for, is because we are not walking in love. Faith that is mixed with love forms compassion in us.

> Galatians 5:6, For in Christ Jesus neither circumcision nor uncircumcision avails anything, but faith working through love.

There is nothing that blocks the blessing and anointing of God from flowing into and through our lives more than strife, bitterness, anger, and hatred.

When we study the lives of great men and women God used in the Bible, one thing is very clear—they were very careful to walk in love.

Even if we operate our faith and do great things for God, if we do not have love, we are nothing.

> 1 Corinthians 13:1-3, Though I speak with the tongues of men and of angels, but have not love, I have become sounding brass or a clanging cymbal. And though I have *the gift of* prophecy, and understand all mysteries

and all knowledge, and though I have all faith, so that I could remove mountains, but have not love, I am nothing. And though I bestow all my goods to feed *the poor,* and though I give my body to be burned, but have not love, it profits me nothing.

When we study the lives of the Patriarchs of our faith, men like Abraham, Isaac, Jacob, and David, we discover they walked in love even when it was difficult for them.

Remember the story of Abraham and Lot? When God called Abraham, his nephew Lot went with him. After a while, the land was filled with their herds, cattle, and servants, and there arose strife between their servants. The news reached Abraham and he called Lot. He said it was not good to have strife and envy between them, so he offered a deal to part ways, and gave Lot first choice of the land.

Lot chose the plain of Jordan and moved toward Sodom and Gomorrah, because those lands were like the garden of the Lord and were well-watered. During the course of time there were wars between different kings of the land. Sodom and Gomorrah were attacked; and Lot, his family, and all of his possessions were taken captive.

Someone informed Abraham about what had happened. Abraham did something unusual for a relative who had left him years before. He chose three hundred and eighteen of his trained servants, who were born in his house, and pursued the king who had taken Lot captive. He did not just send those servants. Abraham went with them to fight, risking his own life and everything he had (Genesis 13 & 14).

That is true love. The Bible says there is no greater love than laying down your life for a friend.

Abraham was not just a man of faith but he was a man of love. Usually we preach about the faith of Abraham but we ignore his life of love.

> John 15:12-14, This is My commandment, that you love one another as I have loved you. Greater love has no one than this, than to lay down one's life for his friends. You are My friends if you do whatever I command you.

Jesus calls us His friends. He showed us an example and laid His life down for us. This is what Abraham did for his nephew Lot, and he was called a friend of God.

He made sure he was walking in love more than running after miracles, power, or anything else he could get from God.

We see the same lifestyle in the sons of Abraham. Isaac laid down his life and was ready to become a sacrifice.

We do not read in the Bible that he put up a temper tantrum when his father said he was going to be sacrificed on the altar.

He loved and trusted his father so much that he was willing to give his life. This is a shadow of the life of Jesus.

Jesus loved His Father so much and He was willing to do anything His Father required of Him, even go to the cross.

Isaac had two sons, Esau and Jacob. At their birth, there was a prophecy that the older would serve the younger. Esau sold his birthright to Jacob for a pot of stew. Jacob also deceived his father and brother to obtain the blessing. His brother was angry and decided to kill Jacob, but Jacob ran away to his mother's people and stayed for many years. Though he was blessed materially, the spiritual blessings did not manifest until the day he decided to reconcile with his brother (Genesis 32).

David is another example of someone who walked in love. When King Saul tried to kill him, David ran from him several times. He could have killed Saul, but did not because of his love for God and respect for his king.

Saul pursued David for almost fourteen years in the wilderness. Finally, God stepped in and recompensed

David for his faithfulness, and he became the greatest king of Israel.

These were men of faith, and if you study their lives, you will see that their faith was mingled with love and God blessed them greatly. Their names became renowned as the names of great men on earth.

When you walk in love, you can be sure that everything else in life will eventually fall into the right place.

3. Faith and Patience

Even if you have all faith, if you do not have the patience to wait for God's timing, you will fail. Just because something is God's will does not mean it is His time for you to do it. Just because you heard from God does not mean you are going to succeed.

The great things in life take a lot of time. Human beings are impatient—we want things to be done in our way and in our time—but I can guarantee that things will not work out that way.

God will test your faith, to see if it passes the tests of time and patience.

> Hebrews 6:11-12, And we desire that each one of you show the same diligence to the full assurance of hope until the end, that you do not become sluggish, but imitate

> those who through faith and patience inherit the promises.

When we study the lives of people God used, we see that they not only had faith, but also patience. Abraham had to wait twenty-five years to see the fulfillment of the promise of a son.

Many of us quit believing God for the things He told us because they did not happen in the time we expected. Rarely will the things God spoke to us happen according to our expectations. God will show up when all hope is lost in the natural; because it will be Him who performs His promise.

Our God is not only a God of faith, but a God of patience:

> Romans 15:5, Now may the God of patience and comfort grant you to be like-minded toward one another, according to Christ Jesus.

In order to preserve our faith and life, patience is an essential quality. If you have faith and love, but do not have patience, you will not achieve much. What is the difference between love and patience?

Patience is enduring love and the ability to wait for the right time. Without it we will not obtain the promise.

> And so, after he had patiently endured, he obtained the promise. (Hebrews 6:15)

If you are interested in learning more about the tests of faith we go through in our lives please order the book "Keys to Fulfilling Your Kingdom Assignment." Please see the last page in this book to know how to place your order.

CHAPTER 5

Putting Your Faith to Work

I already explained about discovering our purpose and how God communicates our purpose to us. The primary way God communicates purpose to His children is through prayer.

In this chapter I want to give a practical explanation and illustration to those steps from life experience.

The Power of Prayer

God has not changed His way of communicating His will to us, which is through prayer.

When I was 16 years old, God began to draw me closer to Him. Though I grew up in a Christian home, I did not know Him. Our home church, though it was almost a hundred years old, was very small, and we had about seven members—four ladies and three men. (I was one of the men.) I wanted to be an electronic engineer because I liked working with electronics. I used to open up the electronic equipment in our home, and I would get in trouble with my Dad for doing so. My father wanted me to be a medical doctor.

When I reached sixteen years of age, something began to change in my life. God began to stir my heart and put a desire for prayer in me, my brother, and another friend of ours.

We would go to the church around eight o'clock at night and pray until four in the morning. When I look back now, that was the best thing that ever happened in my life.

As a result of those prayer times, the focus of our lives began to change. Slowly, He put a desire and a burden in our hearts for His work. We had no idea what we were doing and what prayer was going to do in us.

Gradually, as days, weeks, and months went by, the desire to serve God increased. At the same time, we began to do some evangelistic work, but we did not even have money for public transportation. We collected some gospel tracts and traveled on foot, distributing the tracts wherever we could.

Then, we thought that if we had a bicycle, we could go a little further and reach more people. But we did not have a bicycle, so we prayed to God to give us some money to rent a bicycle on an hourly basis.

The price for an hour was one Indian rupee, which at that time was equivalent to two U.S pennies. The truth was, we did not even have one rupee, so we had to believe God for it.

God provided us with a rupee, and we rented a bicycle from the local store. We owned a ten-watt, battery-operated sound system. We tied that small speaker behind the bicycle and we preached in every town we could.

God began to add more people to our prayer group, but my brother and I, and another relative, were the core group.

If I had not spent that time in prayer, I would not have discovered God's will for my life. How many people forfeit God's perfect will for them because of their lack of prayer?

Why did Jesus spend more time in prayer than doing anything else? He knew that only through prayer could He understand what His Father wanted Him to do. He was giving us an example to follow.

Providing God Substance and Evidence

As we did more evangelism, we were faced with various needs that required answers. As we prayed and did what God told us to do, our faith began to increase. He began to put more of His desires in our hearts.

He prompted us to write down our needs. We did not have a journal or notebook, because we could not afford one, but we had a piece of paper.

> Hebrews 11:1-2, Now faith is the substance of things hoped for, the evidence of things not seen. For by it the elders obtained a *good* testimony.

Many people do not understand how faith works, even though they know by heart what Hebrews 11:1 says.

They neglect two important components of faith, so they do not receive much benefit from their faith.

There are two words that are key in the above verse. They are "substance" and "evidence."

First, the Bible says that faith is the *substance* of things hoped for. The substance of every created thing is the Word of God. He created everything with His Word. God has given us His Word that he used to create everything. If faith is to work, first you need to have the substance, which is the Word of God.

Every time God calls someone, He gives them a promise or an instruction. That promise from God is your spiritual DNA and your inheritance from God as His child.

When we study the people of Israel, we see that when God brought them out of Egypt, He gave them a promise that He was going to take them to a land that flowed with milk and honey.

They were all excited and happy about the promise, but what they did not understand was the *process* to receive the fulfillment of that promise.

After God gives us a promise, He will take us through a process to conform us to His divine nature. As it says in 2 Peter 1:3-4, "As His divine power has given to us all things that *pertain* to life and godliness, through the knowledge of Him who called us by glory and virtue, by which have been given to us exceedingly great and precious promises, that through these you may be partakers of the divine nature, having escaped the corruption *that is* in the world through lust."

After God gave the Israelites the promise, He took them into the wilderness.

The wilderness is the place He takes each of us in order to complete the process. Only if we finish the process will He take us to the Promised Land. Our Promised Land is the destiny each of us has as a child of God.

God takes us through the process is to make sure we really believe His promise and trust Him, regardless of circumstances. Many people fail in the process, just like the people of Israel who perished in the wilderness because of their unbelief.

Another word for process is 'tests.' God gave me a wonderful book, called *Keys to Passing Your Spiritual Tests*, which I recommend you read if you are really serious about fulfilling your purpose.

Not everyone passes the tests in the wilderness. Out of all the people who came out of Egypt, only two passed the wilderness process.

God takes us into the wilderness to be tested. It may not be a literal wilderness, but experiences in which you will be denied the very basic necessities you need for survival, and you will feel like you are going to die.

It is not easy to pass the tests in the wilderness. You will be kept in the wilderness until you learn to live by the Word; until you are so sure, with all of your being, that what God promised is going to come to pass, regardless of how you feel, what you see in the natural, or experience in your immediate circumstances. This is why the Bible says:

> Matthew 4:4, Man shall not live by bread alone, but by every word that proceeds from the mouth of God.

The church has been in the wilderness for almost two thousand years. We love miracles and manifestations and run after them, while we have not possessed the land God has promised us.

The enemy has taken over nations, and almost everything God has given us while we are enjoying the fire by night and cloud by day.

Those are the signs of the wilderness journey. God appointed fire by night and cloud by day to protect and guide His people. When they reached the Promised Land, those signs were not there anymore.

Everything is free in the wilderness; our food, clothing, and water are provided by God. When we reach the Promised Land, we need to produce the things we need ourselves.

The church loves to get free stuff and call it a miracle. Supermarkets from our town in Denver send their expired fruit, bread, and vegetables to churches, because they think we are so helpless and at the bottom of society and can't produce anything.

They treat us like a dumpster where they throw their garbage. Let me tell you, people of God, that is not the real church.

We are supposed to be the most productive people on earth and suppliers of food items to the supermarkets. We are supposed to be the head and not the tail.

This happens because the church has not graduated from the wilderness yet. We are in a season where we must finish our time in the wilderness and then enter the Promised Land.

The chart below will show you where you are at in your life right now:

In the Wilderness	In the Promised Land
God fights for you	God fights in partnership with you
You walk by sight and feeling	You need to walk by faith
God provides for you	You need to produce what you need yourself. God will give you ideas and you need to put these to work by trusting in Him
You will have just enough	You have an abundance
You receive immediate answers to prayer	God builds your faith and patience
You will not fulfill your destiny	The place where you fulfill your destiny
You learn God's ways and wisdom	You apply God's ways and wisdom

In the Wilderness	In the Promised Land
You learn to overcome your flesh	You are led by your spirit
You live by the miracles. Every time God does a miracle you will be happy for the next three days. Then you are crying for the next breakthrough in order to feel that God loves you.	You live by the Word. Man shall not live by bread alone but by every word that comes from the mouth of the Lord. The moment you are ready to live by the Word, you are ready to enter the Promised Land
You live by trusting the power of God	You live by trusting the person and the voice of God
You praise Him because of miracles	You praise Him in spite of your circumstances
A place of tests and preparation	The place of fulfillment

When God called Abraham, He gave him a promise. The next thing Abraham faced in his life was a famine

(Genesis 12:10). That was a wilderness (test) experience for Abraham.

He went down to Egypt and lied on account of his wife. I believe he failed that test, but God did not forsake him.

When we fail a test, God will give us another chance, and keep giving us chances, until we die.

God's ultimate plan for each of us is to be conformed into the image and likeness of His dear Son Jesus Christ (Romans 8:29).

However we have so much 'junk' in us that needs to be burnt up in the fire. Not real fire, but in fiery trials and tests.

Every time we go through fire, a little bit of ungodly nature gets burnt off of us. Depending on how much we cooperate and yield to the process, less or more junk gets burnt off.

If we rebel and disobey, not much junk will get burnt, so He allows us to keep going through the fire again, and longer. But if we yield and comply, more junk gets burnt off and we keep making progress.

Presenting Evidence

Second, you need *evidence*. Do you have any evidence that proves God is going to answer what you are believing Him for?

It is important to write down what you are believing God for. When you write it down, it is evidence that you are really serious and believe that He is going to answer your needs.

God is looking for *substance* and *evidence* in people's lives before He responds to their needs.

We began to dream with God and He put some big desires in our hearts. Then we wrote down the things we needed for doing evangelism.

We needed a good sound system, a vehicle to get around in, and a building for an office, studio, and other ministry purposes.

We drew pictures of the sound system we were believing God for, and the vehicle, and the buildings.

We did not know how any of those things were going to materialize.

In the natural there was no possibility at all. How could we have a vehicle when we had to believe God for two pennies to rent a bicycle?

It will be good if you have a prayer journal. In your prayer journal, write a list of things that you are believing God for this year.

The length of the list is not a problem for God. These should be practical and specific. Please don't write things like, "I want to grow spiritually" or "I would like to have more money" or "Peace" or "Salvation of my loved ones." Those are not specific.

Instead, write things like "I want to pray fifteen minutes every day" or "I would like to have a specific amount of income every month" or "Salvation of _____" and name someone specific. I have thirty-two items on my list for this year.

In each prayer meeting we laid our hands on those needs and commanded them to manifest in the natural realm.

We were all of one heart and one mind. There was no doubt in our hearts.

Not only did we pray for those material needs, we prayed for the sick by faith. We stood and acted like we were praying for the sick, the lame, the blind, and the dead. We would pull people out of wheel chairs, and pull the lame up to walk. These were all done in faith; there were no actual sick people. We were acting as if there were real people.

There was such fervency in our prayers that we were not conscious of time or place.

When I look back now, I understand that God was teaching us something very powerful. He was teaching us how to live by faith.

We never heard anyone teaching us how to live by faith. These things took place from 1988 to 1990.

We never heard any preachers from any other country. We had never read a book on faith other than the Bible.

I can tell you with all honesty that anything we wrote down and prayed in those days, God answered all those prayers, and more than we thought or imagined. Some requests are being fulfilled as I write this book.

We found an almanac of general knowledge, which lists all the countries of the world, and we read the name of each country, and the small description about it, and prayed for those countries. We claimed them for Jesus.

God is now sending me to each of those countries we prayed for, one by one.

More people began to hear about our prayer group and as a result it began to multiply until around twenty, people attended once a week to pray with us.

It was like a small revival broke out among the youth. There was such passion and fervor in our prayer meetings.

No one forced us to pray, no one taught us to pray; it was all done by the Holy Spirit. We had no agenda for how it was going to go or how long it was going to last when we met together. The Holy Spirit took over and we lost awareness of time and space.

Everyone who was part of the core group in those prayer meetings, is in ministry today. As a result, I went to my dad and I cried before him, asking him to send me to a Bible college. At first he hesitated, but the next year he left the decision upto me, and told me to go and do whatever I wanted to do. So when I was eighteen years old, I left my home in Southern India to go to a Bible school in the northern part of India.

I had to travel by train for three days to reach the capital city, and then from there I took a bus to reach the Bible school.

If you know much about India, you are aware that it is a diverse country. South and north are very different in weather, food, language, and culture.

I left my home just like Abraham left his country, kindred, and father's house. I did not know where I was going, but by faith I left.

My father and brother came to the local railway station and sent me off in a train to the capital city.

I was nervous as I did not speak English or Hindi, which is spoken in the northern part of India. I wondered how I was going to reach the Bible school after I got down at the railway station.

There was no one receiving me at the station. I did not know how to ask anyone. But God had already planned all of the details.

There were five other people traveling with me in the train in the same compartment. I was sitting in the middle seat, and there was one person on my left and another person on my right.

After a couple of hours we began to talk and ask about each other. I began to talk to the one on my right. I could not believe what he said, that he was going to the same Bible school as me. I turned to the man on my left, and he said he was the brother of the one sitting on my right and he was going to the same place.

Only God could arrange something like that! Later I found that there were many others on the same train headed to the same Bible school.

When I reached the Bible school, it was like I stepped into my divine destiny. God gave me the English language as a gift, and I began to speak and preach in English within three months. He told me I would need that for my future. At that time, I had no idea what my future was going to be.

Not only did He give me English, I also began to excel in my studies and passed all subjects with A+. During the final year, I was appointed as the leader for the entire student body.

During my second year vacation, a few of us joined together and formed an evangelistic team and rented a home in the nearby town.

As a result of that team work, a church was established, and now there is a big ministry going on in that place with a Christian school and other ministries.

Though I went to the Bible school, I had not yet decided to be in full-time ministry. My main concern was financial support. I did not have anyone supporting me.

My older brother occasionally sent me 500 rupees (about ten dollars) from the stipend he received from the university where he was studying.

My plan was to work and earn some money to do part-time ministry.

I heard about a marine engineering course, and I planned to join that course after my graduation. Because radio marine engineering offered a good salary, and I had to work only six months of the year, with the other six months off from work; I thought it sounded perfect for me. However God had something better in store for me.

It was during the second year of my Bible school that a guest minister came to speak at one of our chapel services.

He was preaching from Genesis chapter fifteen about Abraham. He read from verse one where God said to Abraham, "Do not be afraid, Abram. I am your shield, your exceedingly great reward."

The message this man preached that day hit me like a thunderbolt! I felt like he was pointing his finger at me and talking to me personally. I stood up crying and surrendered my whole life for the work of the Lord. From that day I have never looked back.

Though my financial situation did not change, I had an inner witness that God was going to take care of me.

After my graduation, I joined an evangelistic team and traveled to many states in India, preaching the gospel.

We had to sell gospel tracts and New Testaments to make money to buy food. If we did not sell enough tracts and New Testaments, then we did not have any food.

We were in a state called Uttar Pradesh, where Hinduism was birthed. People were not very interested in buying gospel tracts and New Testaments.

For a week we had only rice, yellow powder, onion, and salt. When we returned to the church we were staying at, we would go and collect firewood and make a stove of rocks. We boiled the rice and mixed the yellow powder, onion, and salt, and ate that for a week.

Your Faith Can Bring Financial Breakthrough

I did not have any revelation about kingdom economy in those days. I was in survival mode and God took care of my needs.

During those evangelistic outreaches, our team had a leader who was a Hindu convert. His family and community ostracized him because he became a Christian and would not even sell anything to him. He did not have money to buy the necessities he needed to survive. We finished a phase of our outreach and prepared to go to our homes for a break. Before we left, this brother asked me a question that changed my financial life forever.

He asked if I would support him with ten rupees per month. At that time ten rupees was only twenty cents USD.

I did not have ten rupees to support him and I did not know what to answer him. I thought for few moments, and the Holy Spirit prompted me in my heart, so I said, "If God gives me ten rupees next month I will send it to you."

I went home and did some work for one of my uncles and he gave me ten rupees. I went to the Post Office and sent a money order to my friend for that amount.

When I stepped out in faith and promised ten rupees when I did not have it, something happened in my life. The spirit of poverty was broken off my life and God told me that I would never run out of money in my pocket. That has been true until today.

It was like the five loaves and two fishes that were given to Jesus; He blessed and fed the five thousand, and had twelve baskets left over.

The next month He gave me thirty rupees, and I sent that to this brother. Every month my income increased and I began to support him every month with one thousand four hundred rupees.

When I look back now, it amazes me what God can do with the little we have.

That brother eventually went to the United States and received his PhD in Theology. He is now serving God in India in a powerful way.

Many people underestimate the power of what they have. They are more conscious of what they don't have than what they have; forgetting that the key to getting what they want is in what they have right now.

You know the stories of the widow in Elijah's time, and what happened to them. As I said earlier, faith is like a coin that has two sides. One is the believing side and the other is the action side. Both sides are required for our faith to work.

The Power of God's Word

The more you read and meditate on God's Word, the better you will hear the voice of God; because when God speaks, He sounds like His Word. The Word is the revealed will of God.

If we have no regard for what is already revealed, then He will not reveal what is hidden.

Once you discover the will of God, then whatever you ask Him according to His will (for your life), He will grant you to your heart's desire.

The reason why many of our prayers are not answered is because we ask amiss, because we are not asking according to His will concerning our life (1 John 5:14).

I would like to share with you an experience I had where the Word of God wrought a miracle in my life.

After graduating from Bible school in India, I joined an evangelistic team and travelled throughout India preaching the gospel from town to town.

During that time, I also had opportunities to attend a couple of conferences conducted by preachers from the United States. This brought a desire in my heart to pursue further studies, but I did not have any money to travel abroad to do so.

Then, my father sent me an application for a Bible school in Denver, Colorado. I applied and they accepted me, but they said I had to pay my tuition because there were no scholarships available that year.

I had to show an $8,000 bank statement to the US Embassy in India for them to approve and issue my visa.

I had only a bank statement for just over $2,000 with me when I went to the Embassy. As I waited in line for my turn to be interviewed, I was nervous and I did not know what was going to happen.

However while I was traveling by train on my way to the embassy, the Lord gave me a word from Proverbs 21:1, which said, "The king's heart *is* in the hand of the Lord, *like* the rivers of water; He turns it wherever He wishes." This verse was the anchor of my faith during the entire trip

When I went to the window to be interviewed, it was a lady that God appointed. She checked my papers and said, "Abraham, you do not have enough money to pay for your tuition. What are you going to do?"

I didn't know what to say, so I didn't say anything. Then she asked a question which I will never forget.

She asked me, "Which is your favorite Psalm in the Bible?" I said, "My favorite Psalm is Psalm 121."

Then she said, "Can you recite it for me?" I said I would. I stood there and said, "I lift up my eyes to the hills from where my help comes, my help comes from the Lord who created heaven and earth." I could only say that much.

Something happened there, and the lady looked at me and said, "You can go."

I got my visa and that is the way I came to the United States for the first time. The rest is history. That is the power of the spoken Word of God.

CHAPTER 6

It is All by Faith

God fulfilled everything that was required to redeem us from every curse, including sickness and disease.

There is nothing remaining on God's part to do for us. Everything concerning our lives was finished and done before the foundation of the earth, and then was manifested through Christ. Now it is up to us to receive it by faith.

The work that we need to do was prepared before the world began (Ephesians 2:10).

The work concerning our future was finished before the foundation of the earth (Ephesians 1:4).

God saved us and called us before time began (2 Timothy 1:9).

We do not need to ask why God is not answering our prayers or how we are going to be healed, or why we cannot have victory in an area of our life. We do not need to ask Him what we need to do? Those are wrong questions.

When the Philippian jailor asked Paul, "What must I do to be saved?" Paul's reply was, "Believe..." (Acts 16:31). There is nothing else you could *do*.

God already answered all of your prayers. God already healed every sickness and disease. God already made you victorious over everything on this earth. He already forgave the sins of the whole world.

That does not mean we do not need to pray for our healing. We just need to learn *how* to pray the right kind of prayer.

If you pay attention to Paul's prayers for the believers, you will notice that he did not pray for their healing and for them to have a bigger house or to be debt free.

His prayer targeted believers receiving a revelation of what God gave them through Christ Jesus. He prayed for the eyes of their understanding to open. He prayed that we would increase in the knowledge of God and His will in all spiritual wisdom and understanding (Ephesians 1:17-21; 3:14-19; Colossians 1:9-12).

When you receive a *revelation* of what is available to you, then you are positioned to receive it by faith.

What we need to do is pray for revelation. Revelation is the unveiling of something that is hidden, in order to bring it to light; to remove the veil so that we can see it clearly.

Once we have revelation, all we need to do is receive by faith what God already made available.

Faith is the foundation of everything in Christian life. We receive salvation by faith. Everything else we need, we also receive by faith.

We remain saved by faith. Once you are saved by grace, you need to make sure you do not get into works to remain saved. Performing good works out of your relationship with God is different than doing good works to remain saved.

You are saved by faith in the One Who saved you, and He is the only One Who is able to keep you from falling. We also live healed and victorious by faith.

We are commanded to live by faith. The Bible says, "The just shall live by faith." **Not just in one place, but in four different places** (Habakkuk 2:4; Romans 1:17; Galatians 3:11; Hebrews 10:38).

Every aspect of life must be lived by faith. Faith is the evidence of things not seen and the assurance of things hoped for (Hebrews 11:1).

Whatever you want to receive that you do not have right now, faith is the evidence and substance for all those things.

We are always asking ourselves what we need to do to get what God has already freely given us. This is why we usually do not receive what we want from God.

We are trying to get healed, we are trying to get blessed, we are trying to get free, etc. All of that *trying* was taken care of on the cross and it is finished.

Through trying, no one can get anything from God. The only means by which we receive anything from God is faith, and faith alone. It is not by trying a little harder.

When we *try* to receive anything from God, we will feel like God is continually raising His bar one notch higher. The next time we try harder, but never seem to reach high enough, and finally, we give up.

It is a religious spirit that keeps us in the rut of the *try harder next time* mentality.

I have been there, and I know what it is like. I was trying to get things from God through good performance, fasting, prayer, being good, shouting louder, and looking as pious as I could, but none of those things impressed God enough to give me anything.

All I needed to do was go to Him in faith in order to receive whatever I needed, and thank Him for it before I received it. He wants to bless me, heal me, and set me free because He loves me, not because I am Mr. Nice.

Many precious believers are trying to be healed. Something in them tells them that if they only did this particular thing, or if they would fast more, or worship God longer, they would get what they need. Those feelings come from the spirit of religion, not from the Holy Spirit.

That religious spirit provokes us to try harder, fast longer, pray more fervently, and worship louder, but never allows us to feel like we have done enough. That is the deception of the enemy.

God does not expect us to do anything in order to receive from Him. All that we need to do is believe He is able, and that He has already done it.

The only thing that impresses God is our faith. The only thing that inspires God to move on our behalf is what we believe. Whatever we do for Him must come out of our love for Him, not from obligation.

We Receive According to Our Faith

It is very important to notice Jesus' response to people when they came to Him expecting to receive a miracle.

He did not say to them, "Let it be according to My ability," or, "Let it be to you according to My anointing."

Jesus didn't exclaim, "Wow! You have been praying for five hours today, let Me heal you!" Or, "My goodness, you have fasted for this for twenty-seven days? I should do this for you." Or, "I know how nice you are; you really deserve it, you earned it."

No. He often said, "Let it be according to your faith." That would be His exact response to you today if you were to go to Jesus, in faith, with your need.

We have to appropriate by faith everything we need in our lives. God has blessed us with all spiritual (whatever comes from God is spiritual) blessings, not some or most of them.

One of the most important things about faith is that it is not a feeling. If it is a feeling, then it is not faith. Those are two different things.

You do not need to *feel* faith. You just need to believe you have faith because the Bible says you do.

I missed God many times because I was looking for the right feeling when I should have simply obeyed what He told me to do.

Read the following scriptures to see what Jesus said concerning faith.

> Matthew 8:10, When Jesus heard it, He marveled, and said to those who followed, "Assuredly, I say to you, I have not found

such **great faith**, not even in Israel!" (emphasis added)

Matthew 9:2, Then behold, they brought to Him a paralytic lying on a bed. When Jesus **saw their faith**, He said to the paralytic, "Son, be of good cheer; your sins are forgiven you." (emphasis added)

Matthew 9:22, But Jesus turned around, and when He saw her He said, "Be of good cheer, daughter; **your faith** has made you well." And the woman was made well from that hour. (emphasis added)

Matthew 9:29, Then He touched their eyes, saying, "According to **your faith** let it be to you." (emphasis added)

Matthew 15:28, Then Jesus answered and said to her, "O woman, great is **your faith**! Let it be to you as you desire." And her daughter was healed from that very hour. (emphasis added)

Mark 10:52, Then Jesus said to him, "Go your way; **your faith** has made you well." And immediately he received his sight and followed Jesus on the road. (emphasis added)

Luke 7:50, Then He said to the woman, "**Your faith** has saved you. Go in peace." (emphasis added)

> Luke 17:19, And He said to him, "Arise, go your way. **Your faith** has made you well." (emphasis added)

All of the above Scriptures, and more, tell me one thing: It is not according to Jesus or what He is able to do; the most important component to receiving what I need is what I believe in my heart.

Let me tell you this: what you believe in your heart will eventually manifest in your life. What you keep meditating on in your heart will eventually become your reality. No one can do anything for you unless you change your reality by believing differently.

Many precious believers live their life wishing God would do something for them. Most die wishing but they never move beyond wishing to the point of belief. They think it is up to God to do everything for them.

Let me tell you the good news: God has already done it. It is up to us now to receive it.

The Bible says God is able to do more than we could ask or imagine according to the power that is working in us (Ephesians 3:20). God is able to do exceedingly abundantly all that we ever ask or imagine, not according to Him or His power, but the *power of faith* that is working in us daily. So:

- It is by faith we become a child of God.

- It is by faith we receive our salvation.
- It is by faith we receive our healing.
- It is by faith we receive our financial blessing.
- It is by faith we overcome the enemy.
- It is by faith we overcome the world.
- It is by faith we fight the good fight of faith.
- It is by faith we have been made righteous.
- It is by faith we have been justified.
- It is by faith we have received the Holy Spirit.
- It is by faith we love one another.
- It is by faith we believe in God, and that He is a rewarder of those who diligently seek Him.
- It is by faith we trust in God.
- It is by faith we receive whatever we need.
- It is by faith we walk, not by sight.

Faith. Faith. Nothing more than faith. If there is no faith, there is frustration and misery. When there is faith, there is victory, joy, and abundance.

Dear child of God, if you get this into your heart, you get everything. But if you do not get this in your heart, you will get *nothing*.

If you are sick in your body or poor financially, do not ever think that if God wants to heal you or bless you He will do it.

No, it is not *if* God wants it, it is if *you* want it; and if you believe that God has done it for you, then you will receive it. Otherwise, forget about it.

Jesus was not running around healing everyone who sat at home and wished they were healed. He healed only those people who came to Him in faith, and believed that He was willing and able to heal them. They received their healing.

What do you believe in your heart today? Do you believe God is able to meet your need? Or, do you feel like you need to do something more to be ready to be healed?

No, it is simple faith; faith that is as old as the heaven and earth and, if you belong to God, He gave you enough faith to believe for anything—as long as you are willing.

We all go through our season of the test of faith, but that is not permanent. The moment you speak something positive with your mouth, you are releasing the faith you have.

The good news is that you can do this at any time; it is your choice. The more you speak positive things, the more faith you will have.

The opposite is also true. The less you speak positive things with your mouth; the less faith you will have. It is all up to you!

IT IS ALL BY FAITH

> Mark 11:23, For assuredly, I say to you, whoever says to this mountain, 'Be removed and be cast into the sea,' and does not doubt in his heart, but believes that those things he says will be done, he will have whatever he says.

The verse above says we shall have whatever we say.

I lived in a religious rut for most of my life, wishing that someday God would do something great for me; wishing that someday I would feel better; wishing that someday I would be happy; wishing that someday I would overcome my challenges.

I waited thirty-five years and those things did not come. But when I received the revelation of faith, what I had been waiting thirty-five years for came in one split second, and I never looked back.

God opened my eyes to see that the just shall live by faith. If we are not living by faith, we are wasting our time and our lives.

If we are not living by faith, we are not pleasing God. If we are not living by faith, we are not being fruitful.

When we do not live by faith, we are committing sin. The Bible says that whatsoever does not originate in faith is sin (Romans 14:23).

Before this experience, I spent my life wishing I had more faith. I used to think to myself, "I wish I had faith like so and so." That was the wrong confession.

Instead, I should have said I had faith, whether it was little or much. As I said earlier, the more I made positive confessions; the more my faith grew. It was all up to me.

Most Christians live their lives like God has not done a good job saving them. They live like they are half-saved. Or, they live like they are good for nothing on this earth, and are just waiting to go to heaven.

God will let you live in your misery as long as you want. Whatever you want from God, believe that He has already done it for you, and you will have it. That is God's Word, and it is guaranteed.

> Mark 11:24, Therefore I [Jesus] say to you, whatever things you ask when you pray, believe that you receive them, and you will have them.
>
> Matthew 21:22, And whatever things you ask in prayer, believing, you will receive.

Whether you believe it or not, you have faith. It is your choice to believe it or not to believe it. God will not force belief upon you.

God has no limit, but we limit Him by what we believe and what we say.

There is another perfect example in the gospels that shows us the power of our faith.

One day a father brought his son to the disciples to heal him. They did all they could (I have been there) and this boy was not healed:

> Mark 9:14-19, And when He [Jesus] came to the disciples, He saw a great multitude around them, and scribes disputing with them. Immediately, when they saw Him, all the people were greatly amazed, and running to Him, greeted Him.
>
> And He asked the scribes, "What are you discussing with them?" Then one of the crowd answered and said, "Teacher, I brought You my son, who has a mute spirit. And whenever it seizes him, it throws him down; he foams at the mouth, gnashes his teeth, and becomes rigid. So I spoke to Your disciples, that they should cast it out, but they could not."
>
> He answered him and said, "O faithless generation, how long shall I be with you? How long shall I bear with you? Bring him to Me."

The reason the disciples could not cast out this demon was because they did not believe they could do it. They were *trying* to heal this person.

The following verses explain the solution:

> Mark 9:20-24, Then they brought him to Him. And when he saw Him, immediately

the spirit convulsed him, and he fell on the ground and wallowed, foaming at the mouth.

So He asked his father, "How long has this been happening to him?" And he said, "From childhood. And often he has thrown him both into the fire and into the water to destroy him. **But if You can do anything,** have compassion on us and help us."

Jesus said to him, "**If you can believe, all things are possible to him who believes.**" Immediately the father of the child cried out and said with tears, "Lord, I believe; help my unbelief!" (emphasis added)

The father finally brought his son to Jesus and asked Him—if He could do something—to please heal his son. That is the wrong thing to ask God.

Jesus replied and told him it is not a question of *if* God can do something; it is whether you are able to believe God can accomplish what you are believing for.

God meets our needs according to the level of our faith. The blessings we receive from God are directly proportionate to the faith we have in God, not according to the ability or power of God.

The faith we have in God's ability creates the miracle we need.

God is always ready and willing to act on our behalf. We must prepare our hearts by removing all unbelief and doubt.

Let us see from the Word of God how faith works.

We see in the Gospels the woman with the issue of blood who suffered with that sickness for twelve long years. She did everything she could to get healed from her plague, but was not cured.

That means she "tried" everything she could, as you and I do sometimes, to get healed.

She might have wished all those years to be healed. She might have wished God heard her prayers. She might have thought she was not worthy to be healed. She might have thought God did not love her enough; for if He really did, He would have healed her.

She spent all of her money getting medical help from different doctors, but nothing changed her situation.

One day she heard something. She heard about the man called Jesus, and that He healed the sick:

> Mark 5:25-29, Now a certain woman had a flow of blood for twelve years, and had suffered many things from many physicians. She had spent all that she had and was no better, but rather grew worse.

> When **she heard about Jesus,** she came behind Him in the crowd and touched His garment. **For she said, "If only I may touch His clothes, I shall be made well."** Immediately the fountain of her blood was dried up, and she felt in her body that she was healed of the affliction. (emphasis mine)

She might not have known who Jesus was. She might not have had all the right theology or prayed in tongues seven hours a day to be built up in her spirit. She might not have even gone to church [temple] for the last twelve years, because a woman with such a sickness was not allowed in public.

I could go on and on explaining her situation, and I can guarantee that it was much worse than I can describe.

One day something happened; someone came and told her about Jesus. When she heard the news about Him, something erupted in her heart—faith! When faith came into her heart, she did something. She began to *say* that she was going to be healed.

> Mark 6:56, Wherever He entered, into villages, cities, or the country, they laid the sick in the marketplaces, **and begged Him that they might just touch the hem of His garment. And as many as touched Him were made well."** (emphasis added)

IT IS ALL BY FAITH

What actually healed her was what she said; because Jesus said, "We shall have whatsoever we say" (Mark 11:23). She took her healing by force even without Jesus' prior knowledge.

What was not made possible in twelve years of *trying* was made possible in one moment. That is the difference between trying in our own strength to get something from God, and receiving from God by faith.

The Bible says that the more she tried, the worse her situation grew. The more she tried, the more money she had to spend for her treatment. The Bible says she spent all that she had and went to many physicians.

Faith comes by hearing and hearing comes by the Word of God (Romans 10:17).

The power of faith is one of the greatest forms of power on this earth. When you hear the Word of God, it brings forth faith in you.

Every word that you receive from God carries the needed amount of faith to fulfill that word. It can move any mountain and change any situation.

You can be free from any problem in your life. You can be healed of any sickness. Jesus paid the whole price; now it is up to us to believe it.

Do not wait around for God to do something about your problem. He already did everything for you. You go to Him in faith and receive it.

The Bible says,

> Romans 8:32, He who did not spare His own Son, but delivered Him up for us all, how shall He not with Him also *freely* give us all things? (emphasis added)

Whatever God gives us is free. We do not need to pay anything. All we need is faith.

There was a time I believed God blesses us according to His ability and power, and now I know that is not true. God blesses us based on the *size* of our faith.

I used to be like the brother of the prodigal son, who lived in his father's house like a servant but never enjoyed a blessing. His belief was that his father did not want him to enjoy any blessing. His understanding was that if his father wanted to bless him, he would really bless him; he did not need to ask.

He could not accept the fact that his younger brother, who left home and spoiled the wealth of his father, came back and was enjoying his father's blessings. I believe the greatest revelation he ever had in his life was when his father said to him, "Son you are always with me and all that I have is yours." (Luke 15:31)

Many precious believers are like that. They think that if God wants to bless them, He will bless them.

There are others who try and try and work hard to earn the blessings from God; when, the whole time, all that their Father had was theirs to enjoy.

No, dear friend, even though God has all the blessings you need, He will not just bless you unless you believe and ask Him.

The Bible says we do not have because we do not ask (James 4:2). I have found that we ask, based on our faith in God's goodness. If our faith is big, we will ask big; if our faith is small, we will ask small. We decide the size of our asking and we decide the size of our blessings.

Contending for Your faith

Because our faith is the most holy substance and is very precious, the enemy wants to steal it or defile it.

We need to learn to contend for our faith as the Bible says in Jude 3, "Beloved, while I was very diligent to write to you concerning our common salvation, I found it necessary to write to you exhorting you to contend earnestly for the faith which was once for all delivered to the saints."

The enemy wants to steal, corrupt, or nullify your faith so that you are not a threat to his kingdom. The question is, how do we contend for our faith?

We fight the good fight of faith.

How do we fight the good fight of faith?

It is with the sword of the Spirit, which is the Word of God.

When Jesus was tempted by the Devil, He used the Word to defeat the Satan.

When the Word is being preached, the devil comes to steal the Word from the hearts of people (Mark 4:15; Luke 8:12).

You and I have the mind of Christ, and the mind of Christ operates according to the Word of God.

Any time a negative thought comes to your mind, you confront it with the Word of God. That is how you contend for your faith.

Refuse to entertain negative thoughts and thoughts of failure, defeat, and destruction. These are not from God.

Any time you speak negative words, you are nullifying your faith. Any time you speak positive words, you are building up your faith.

The most dangerous warfare is the warfare of your faith. There is a battle going on every moment against your faith. You may not even realize it.

This is why the Bible says to be vigilant, or watchful, and pray (1 Peter 5:8). It also says to examine yourself to know whether you are in faith:

2 Corinthians 13:5, **Examine** yourselves *as to* whether you are in the faith. Test yourselves. Do you not know yourselves, that Jesus Christ is in you?—unless indeed you are disqualified.

I pray that this book has been a blessing to you. If you need more copies of this or other books we have, please do not hesitate to contact us.

Questions

Use additional paper as needed.

1. Explain an experience when you stepped out in faith to obey what God told you to do:

_____

_____

_____

_____

_____

2. Describe and explain an incident where you missed God, or you did not do; what He asked you to do and the reason why?

_____

_____

_____

_____

_____

3. Based on Romans 12:6-8, what gifts did you receive when you were Born Again?

_____

_____

_____

_____

_____

4. Describe and explain a time when a gift of the Holy Spirit operated through you.

_____

_____

_____

_____

5. Describe and explain the experience surrounding your salvation.

_____

_____

_____

_____

6. Were you ever disappointed in God? When you look back at that incident, what is your perception now?

QUESTIONS

7. Explain the most crucial test or trial of your faith that you faced in your life based on 1 Peter 1:7. How did you manage your faith during that time?

More Books & Resources

DISCIPLING NATIONS SERIES

Kingdom Mandate (for any donation)

Discovering the Lost Kingdom (Volume 1) $14.00

Purpose, Calling, and Gifts (Volume 2) $15.00

God's Original Design (Volume 3) $20.00

Seeing, Entering, and Manifesting the Kingdom of God (Volume 4) $20.00

The Ekklesia (Volume 5) $30.00

The Gospel of the Kingdom (Volume 6) $20.00

Power and Authority of the Church (Volume 7) $15.00

Kingdom Family (Volume 8) $15.00

The Birthing of a Kingdom Nation (Volume 9) $20.00

What Happened to God? (Volume 10) $20.00

7 Dimensions and Operations of the Kingdom of God (Volume 11) $15.00

Kingdom Economy (Volume 12) $15.00

Kingdom Government (Volume 13) $15.00

Releasing Kings and Queens to their Original Intent (Volume 14) $10.00

Kingdom Secrets to Restoring Nations Back to God (Volume 15) $20.00

Keys to Fulfilling Your Kingdom Assignment (Volume 16) $15.00

KINGDOM LIVING SERIES

The Three Most Important Decisions of Your Life $15.00

Recognizing God's Timing for Your Life $12.00

Overcoming the Spirit of Poverty $10.00

Seven Kinds of Believers $10.00

7 Dimensions of God's Glory $5.00

7 Dimensions of God's Grace $10.00

7 Kinds of Faith $7.00

KINGDOM BOOKS FOR KIDS

Genesis 126 Three Volume Book set for boys $25.00

TO PLACE AN ORDER:

www.TheKingdomNetwork.org
Phone: 1-800-558-5020
Email: info@TheKingdomNetwork.org

Are you struggling to discover your **PURPOSE ?**
You are not supposed to fit in but stand out !

Sign up today for the
FREE Online Kingdom Course

DISCOVERING

THE LOST KINGDOM

In this course you'll DISCOVER:

>> Your true identity and purpose
>> What God is doing on the earth and how you can partner with Him in it
>> Why God created the earth and put us on this planet
>> And much more ...

Why are people becoming more and more disinterested in **church and religion** globally?
Join the course, and discover
what your soul has been searching for all along.

FREE BOOK AND STUDY GUIDE

Other courses available
>> DISCOVERING PURPOSE, CALLING AND GIFTS
>> SEEING, ENTERING AND MANIFESTING THE KINGDOM
>> GOD'S ORIGINAL DESIGN
>> The Ekklesia
>> The Next move of GOD
   And more ...

Register Now @ **www.TheKingdomUniversity.org**

Welcome to
KINGDOM DELIVERANCE
— WORKSHOP —

**Are you tired of waiting and looking for breakthroughs?
Kingdom of God has the answer.**

This kingdom deconstruct workshop is divided into EIGHT major categories which deal with the eight major areas of our life. Each one is connected to the next, and so if one of these areas dysfunctions, it will affect all other areas of your life.

1. Relationship with the Father
2. Spiritual Healing
3. Emotional Healing
4. Recognizing Purpose and Calling
5. Identifying and Mastering Natural and Spiritual Gifts
6. Finances—Learning to Live in Kingdom Economy
7. Healing Relationships
8. Physical Health

*Take action now.
Order all 8 workshop manuals today !*

Thank you so much for taking the courses from The Kingdom University. Taking a course is only the first step. We are pleased to present you with the next step—that of going through the process to get rid of all the extra weights that have been slowing and hindering you from fully living out your kingdom assignment.

Call 1 800 558 5020   www.TheKingdomNetwork.org

www.ingramcontent.com/pod-product-compliance
Lightning Source LLC
Chambersburg PA
CBHW070121080526
44586CB00013B/1349